In My
Father's
VINEYARD

In My Father's VINEYARD

WAYNE JACOBSEN

Adapted by Anne Christian Buchanan

WORD PUBLISHING
Dallas·London·Vancouver·Melbourne

Published by Word Publishing, Inc., Dallas, Texas 75234

All Scripture quotations in this book are from the *New International Version of the Bible* (NIV), copyright © 1983 by the International Bible Society. Used by permission of Zondervan Bible Publishers.

The material in this book was adapted from *The Vineyard,* © 1991 Wayne Jacobsen. Other books by Wayne Jacobsen include the following: *The Naked Church, Tales of the Vine,* and *Pathways of Grace.*

Wayne Jacobsen, a church leader, writer, and teacher for more than 20 years, resides in Visalia, California. He conducts seminars on intimacy with God and church renewal through Lifestream Ministries.

Project conception and coordination by Mason Wheeler Communications, Eugene, Oregon.

J. Countryman is a registered trademark of Word Publishing, Inc.

A J. Countryman Book

Designed by Garborg Design Works, Minneapolis, Minnesota.

Photography by Bob Sogge, AFP

Project Editor — Terri Gibbs

ISBN: 0-8499-5296-4

Printed and bound in the United States of America

7 8 9 0 1 2 3   RRD   9 8 7 6 5 4 3 2 1

To:

DAVE AND DONNA COLEMAN

GAYLE AND ADA ERWIN

JACK AND NANCY GERRY

BOB AND JAY LANNING

CHUCK AND RUBY SHOEMAKE

KEVIN AND VAL SMITH

You picked us up when we were broken;

you held us up when the darkness engulfed us;

and you gave us room to heal in the Father's love.

You showed us what true friends are like,

demonstrated what it means to put obedience

to the Father above the understanding and accolades

of other people, and by doing so taught us

what it really means to bear

the fruit of the Father's vineyard.

CONTENTS

I have called you friends,

for everything that

I learned from my Father

I have made known to you.

JOHN 15:15

CHAPTER

*I am
the vine…*

JOHN 15:5

AN INVITATION

THIS IS MY FAVORITE time of the year in the vineyard. It is only mid-February, but in the short winters of California's San Joaquin Valley, spring is just around the corner. The ever-lengthening days are already clawing at winter's grip, and soon it will succumb.

It is almost evening. Lights from distant farmhouses have already begun to twinkle against the subdued landscape, and out of the diaphanous shroud of evening fog, rows of grapevines curve over the hills and completely surround me.

All the vines are neatly trimmed, their branches gently twisting around the wire strung from posts that stand in tidy rows. Everything here is at rest now, patiently awaiting the glory of springtime—and another cycle of fruitfulness.

Only a few months ago the air was filled with dust, voices, and the churning tractor engines that marked the frenzied drive to harvest the grapes before the first rain. But now it is quiet, and though a glance from a distant farmhouse might lead someone to believe that I am alone, it is not so, for I have come here to walk and talk with the Father.

This vineyard has been my cherished prayer closet since I

was a young boy. No place on earth more quickly draws me to God, because it was here that we first met. This is where I learned to walk with him, to hear his voice and surrender my life to his will.

This is my father's vineyard—the thirty-five acre vineyard where I was raised. Here, season after season, my father grows grapes to dry and sell as raisins. Ever since I can remember, this place has been my father's tool—not only to provide for his family but, more importantly, to teach his four sons about God and his ways. Since the vineyard is where I learned the most about God and about life, it is no wonder to me that when Jesus wanted to reveal the secrets of the kingdom to his followers he, too, chose a vineyard for his teaching tool. On that long-ago evening, when he wanted to tell them how to live fruitful lives of rich personal fulfillment, where did he take them?

To a vineyard.

To his Father's vineyard.

"I am the true vine," he told them.

> *Sing about a
> fruitful vineyard:
> I, the LORD,
> watch over it;
> I water it
> continually.
> I guard it day
> and night
> so that no one
> may harm it.*
>
> ISAIAH 27:2–3

Perhaps Jesus spotted a small stand of vines near the Garden of Gethsemane. I can see him walking over to a grapevine, affectionately taking one of the tender, young canes in his hand and inviting his disciples to gather around as he launched into one of the most intriguing stories of his ministry.

Jesus took his disciples to the vineyard, and that is where he takes us as well. So let's go to the vineyard together, you and I. Let's walk the rows with our Father. Let's listen in the still of the morning, in the calm of the evening as he teaches us the lessons of the vineyard and shows us how to find the fulfillment he has promised to every believer.

Including me.

Including you!

Come. . .

This Is My Father's Vineyard

THERE HAS NEVER been any doubt in my mind that this is my father's vineyard.

Throughout my adolescent years, I frequently questioned my father's ideas and decisions, but I never questioned him when it came to the vineyard. Whatever he said went. He knew best how to make the vineyard thrive.

My father was part of a passing generation of family farmers. He cared for his own vines, refusing to buy more land than he could farm himself. While many farmers hired out the work or even rented out the entire vineyard to someone else, my father was extremely reluctant to bring others into his vineyard. He hired help only for the work he could not possibly do himself, and that with great apprehension.

Naturally, no one he hired ever met his exacting standards—because no one cared for the vineyard as much as he did. I've seen the disappointed look in his eye when raisins were carelessly strewn on the ground. I've felt his pain when he gazed at a vine I had carelessly pruned.

In my father's vineyard there was never any doubt who was in charge, who cared most deeply.

I am the true vine, and my Father is the gardener.

JOHN 15:1

The same is true in God's vineyard. Jesus is the true Vine, we are the branches, and our heavenly Father is the Owner and the Gardener. That means, of course, that God is in charge. He can do what he pleases in the vineyard. We who are merely branches, or even we who labor in his vineyard, have no right to question his decisions.

Regrettably, there are times when I spend the bulk of my prayer life trying to counsel God to resolve my situation in the way I imagine is best. Foolishly, I forget that this is my Father's vineyard. He knows what he is doing, and he has a right to do what he wants to.

Lest that sound harsh or frightening, remember that God is more than just the One in charge. He is also the Husbandman who cares tenderly for his vineyard. He is the God of loving compassion whose mercies never fail.

When we are in pain, when we can't see a way out, when the days drag by without solutions, he comes to us with tenderness and incredible love. This Gardener can take any branch, no matter how wounded, and put it back together again. It may not be a quick fix. It may take awhile, but the Father has grace enough to forgive our failures and strength enough to transform any crisis.

This is my Father's vineyard. He's in charge.

He cares for us deeply and tenderly.

He provides everything we need to grow and be fruitful.

Isn't that a Gardener you can trust?

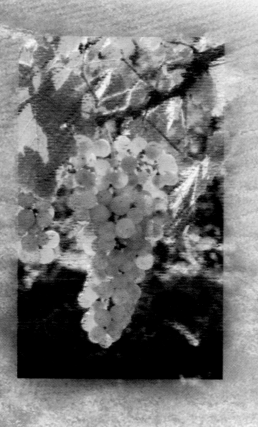

CHAPTER

3

VINES AND BRANCHES

I am the vine;
you are the
branches....
I have called
you friends.

JOHN 15:5, 15

FEW PLANTS COME IN as many fascinating shapes as grapevines. Their trunks twist up from the ground in a myriad of shapes and forms. Two feet or so above ground the trunk separates into craggy arms that continue the seemingly random twisting and turning as they reach toward the wires above. One of our favorite games as children was to challenge each other to impersonate a chosen grapevine by contorting our own trunk and limbs to match it.

Thinking back, though, I can't remember ever making much of a distinction between the vine and the branch. The same rough, flaky bark that starts just above ground continues up the gnarled, twisted trunk to where it separates into craggy arms and on up to where the slender, flexible canes emerge.

There is no fixed line that says the vine ends here and the branch begins there. That is why Jesus couldn't have chosen a better illustration of the intimate bond he seeks with his followers. He wants us to identify so closely with him that others cannot tell where he leaves off and where we begin.

No branch has any life in itself; only the Vine does. A branch must draw life from the Vine, for without him nothing will ultimately satisfy.

Who has not sought out a new job, home, or other possession, certain that it would fulfill a deep longing, only to find that its joy quickly faded? How many of our relationships are so loaded with expectations of what other people should provide for us that we're constantly disappointed when they fall short?

Jesus made clear at the outset of this parable that he was not just a vine, but the *true* Vine. He described this incredible relationship by declaring: "I have called you friends."

Now take everything you know about a good friendship, picking the best you've ever experienced, and you'll understand the wonder of Jesus' invitation to you. He wants to be the best Friend you've ever had—sharing every moment of your life. He wants to laugh with you, even through your slips and spills. He wants to relax with you in your weariness, to commune with you on the issues that affect you most.

The fulfillment and fruitfulness Jesus offered is found only in friendship with him. It is the essence of life in God's vineyard.

He is the true Vine.

We are the branches, drawing nourishment from him. Enjoying him.

He is our true Friend.

There is no life without him.

CHOSEN BRANCHES

IN MY FATHER'S FIELDS, the branches grow naturally out of the vine. First comes the vine, rooted sturdily in the ground. Then come the branches, the canes, the leaves, and finally the fruit. Although the process requires some cultivation, it is perfectly normal.

But it doesn't always happen that way.

Sometimes, instead of growing naturally from the vine, branches are grafted into the vine.

Grafting is a nearly miraculous process in which one new plant is made out of two different ones. A branch is taken from one vine and inserted into a cut on another vine. The branch is bound to the new vine with an adhesive compound or tape. As the "wound" heals, the two plants become one, the new branch drawing sap from the roots of the established vine.

In a sense, this is a more accurate picture of our relationship with the Vine in God's vineyard than the ordinary process of growth. We didn't just grow there. We were grafted, joined to Christ out of his own loving initiative.

Jesus told the disciples, "You did not choose me, but I chose you."

Chosen.

You did not choose me, but I chose you.

JOHN 15:16

It was that simple.

The disciples had not come to Christ by their own determination or because they just happened to be at the right place at the right time. Their participation in his life was not a random act of nature. The true Vine had chosen them to be grafted into him—and he has chosen us as well.

Chosen. It's a humbling but comforting word.

Anyone who has ever waited in line only to be the last chosen for a team knows the terrifying humiliation of not being wanted. When we are grafted into Christ, we never have to know that humiliation again. There is no greater assurance than knowing that Jesus has chosen you and me to be grafted into him. Yet his choosing does not exclude anyone else. On this Vine there is room for everyone.

No matter how unloved you have felt in the past, no matter how lost you feel in your sin, God knew all of that when he chose you—and he wants you anyway.

Hope for finding fulfillment in God's vineyard springs from this simple truth: *He wants you to be grafted onto his Vine, to draw your life from him.*

When it comes down to our relationship with Jesus, isn't that what really matters?

If . . . you, though a

wild olive shoot,

have been grafted in

among the others and

now share in the

nourishing sap

from the olive root,

do not boast over those

branches. If you do,

consider this:

You do not support

the root, but the root

supports you.

ROMANS 11:17–18

5

If a man remains in me and I in him, he will bear much fruit; apart from me you can do nothing.

JOHN 15:5

IF...

I'VE SEEN IT HAPPEN a thousand times—and each time it seems such a waste.

A branch will look fine and healthy, but the canes that spring from it are withered and sickly. Few if any of them will ever reach up to the wire intended to support them. There's not even a chance that fruit will spring from such a branch.

Such a waste. It takes many years for a branch to develop, and each branch holds the potential for bearing fruit, yet when it is obvious that a branch is no longer capable of bearing fruit, it has to be cut off.

As I pruned the vines in my father's vineyard, I had total freedom to shape them any way I chose. I decided which branches would remain and which would be cut off. The branches had nothing to say about it, no volition of their own.

But here the Father's vineyard takes a major departure from our earthly ones, for in his vineyard the branches have their own will. He does not compel them to grow there. Each branch must choose whether to be part of the Vine or not.

Jesus explained this truth to his disciples with a simple two-letter word: *if.*

Five times he used that simple word to highlight the role the branch plays in being part of God's vineyard.

"If a man remains in me and I in him, he will bear much fruit."

"If anyone does not remain in me, he is like a branch that is thrown away and withers."

"If you remain in me and my words remain in you, ask whatever you wish, and it will be given you."

"If you obey my commands, you will remain in my love."

"You are my friends if you do what I command."

If—it's a simple word to state simple realities.

If we want to be part of God's vineyard, we have to participate in the life of the Vine. That choice is not whether we want to be fulfilled in God's life or whether we want to be fruitful for his kingdom. The choice is whether or not we will accept his offer of friendship by remaining in him.

If we do, he offers a dazzling array of opportunities to each of us. If not, we must face certain judgment. The branch dries up and is thrown away. Why? Because "apart from me you can do nothing." When we cut ourselves off from relationship with Jesus, we cannot bear fruit in God's kingdom.

How I wish this were as clear in the spiritual vineyard as it is in the earthly one! The moment a branch is cut off from the life-giving nourishment of the vine it begins to wither. Almost immediately the leaves begin to sag, and though they may still be green, their limpness is a sure sign that death has already come.

Neglecting a vital friendship with Jesus is one of the gravest dangers to spiritual well-being, and it can happen so subtly, because we are easily distracted from him by the challenges and opportunities of our culture. We may still be engrossed in a wide variety of religious activities. And his blessing may still seem to accompany us even as we get by on our own strength, unaware of the creeping death that has been unleashed. Then one day we wake up feeling empty or stressed by the demands on our lives. We wonder why God doesn't seem as close to us as before, never recognizing that *we* have drawn back from the Vine.

Apart from Christ there will be no fruit—and there will be no joy.

In Christ, there is true life, full and abundant.

If.

If what?

If we choose to remain in him, firmly grafted into the Vine.

6

LOVE FOR THE LONG HAUL

ON A GRAPEVINE, the only difference between a cane and a branch is longevity.

A *cane* is a new shoot, the product of one season.

A *branch* is a part of the vine that has been there for a long time. Its ability to transform the nourishment of the vine into a harvest of grapes results from many years of continued attachment to the vine.

Some of the branches in my father's vineyard are more than forty years old, and yet they continue to yield one bountiful harvest after another. Vineyards are long-term crops, with mature vines producing far more than young ones.

God wants us to be long-term residents in his vineyard as well. His goal for us is fruitful maturity. That's why Jesus said it was so important for us to remain in him.

Remain. He repeats the word throughout his lesson on the vineyard—ten times in fact.

Remain in me.

That simple response is all Jesus asks of the branches in God's vineyard.

> *As the Father has loved me, so have I loved you. Now remain in my love.*
>
> JOHN 15:9

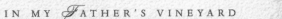

The interdependence of the branch with the grapevine is an ideal picture of our relationship with Christ. We are not just staying with him, standing nearby, watching what's going on. We are linked to him, grafted to him. Our identity and existence are bound up in him.

And what Jesus asks of us, he offers to us as well. Twice in this very passage he tells us that he will remain in us also. Not only will we live in him, but he will live in us—and the relationship we have with him will be as close as the one he shares with the Father. "You will remain in my love, just as I remain in his love."

What a marvelous promise. What a fantastic relationship to pursue! Growing in it will be a lifetime adventure. All we have to do is stay in the Vine where the Father grafted us.

What a contrast to everything this world teaches us: if we want anything in this life we must achieve it, investing our energies to somehow gain what we desire. But in God's vineyard, we don't have to achieve anything. When God established us in Christ, he gave us a gift of friendship, regenerating our hearts, making us sensitive to his presence and his voice. All we need to do now is embrace that friendship and not run off at every distraction or be pulled away by every temptation.

Remaining in him is as simple as regularly being where he is. Jesus doesn't hide from his followers, but clearly tells us where to find him—in his Word, in prayer, in our surrender to him, in the lives of other believers, and in serving people who are in need.

"Remain in my love." How much more simply could Jesus have said it? No matter what the challenge, no matter how right your perspective may appear, invest your trust in him—today, and every day for the rest of your life. Then you will know the depth of lifelong friendship. You will know a security that can win over misunderstood suffering, unanswered prayers, months of unemployment, or the loss of friends.

Remain in him. That's all he asks us to do. Amidst the struggles and fears, the confusions and doubts, remain grafted to the Vine.

And we can remain in his love forever, for that love will never let us go.

ACCORDING TO SEASON

*As long as
the earth
endures,
seedtime and
harvest, cold
and heat,
summer and
winter, day
and night will
never cease.*

GENESIS 8:22

WITHOUT THE CHANGING SEASONS, vineyards would never bear fruit. Each season offers something the vine needs for continued growth. Spring brings rain and softened days to gently stimulate the growth that will come to full maturity in the vibrant warmth of summer. Autumn is the time of harvest, and winter brings a much-needed rest and restaging to the vine. Without this rest, the vine would not be strong enough to go through the cycle again to harvest.

The ever-changing seasons also determine the tasks of the farmer in the vineyard. If he tries to gather grapes in spring, he will find only the smallest beginnings of a harvest still to come. If he tries to prune in summer, he will destroy the vine he is committed to care for.

Would it be fair for us to assume there are also seasons in the Father's vineyard? Ecclesiastes states it simply: "There is a time for everything, and a season for every activity under heaven."

God works with us at different times in different ways. Sometimes our lives seem to bubble over with joy; at every turn we see God's hand moving. At other times, needs press us from all sides. We find ourselves repenting far more often than rejoicing.

If we don't understand that God works in seasons, we'll make the mistake of assuming that the moments of euphoria are what Christianity is meant to be, that anything less is a source of continual condemnation.

Without the changing seasons, vineyards would never bear fruit. Likewise, our spiritual growth demands an ever-changing climate—seasons when God's work is tailor-made to our personal circumstances. Seasons designed by the Father as he nourishes our lives toward fruitfulness. Seasons that bring a healthy balance of joy and challenge, of diligent effort and renewing rest.

We must learn not only to embrace the season we're in, to enjoy its gifts and confront its challenges, but also to let it go when the seasons change.

The cycle of God's care is always dependable. Even when we can't see it, he is working to bring fruit in our lives. The key to remaining in the Vine is to look for the way God is working in our lives at any given moment.

It's God's vineyard, remember. He determines the seasons of our lives—when to prune, when to feed, or when to harvest.

We are the branches on his Vine, privileged to grow and blossom and bear fruit—to follow his perfect plan through all the seasons of our lives.

> *As the rain and the snow come down from heaven, and do not return to it without watering the earth and making it bud and flourish, so that it yields seed for the sower and bread for the eater, so is my word that goes out from my mouth: It will not return to me empty, but will accomplish what I desire and achieve the purpose for which I sent it.*
>
> ISAIAH 55:10–11

PART TWO:

See! The winter is past;

the rains are over and gone.

Flowers appear on the earth;

the season of singing

has come, the cooing of doves

is heard in our land.

The fig tree forms its early fruit;

the blossoming vines

spread their fragrance.

SONG OF SONGS 2:10–13

CLEAN AND NEW

*You are
already clean
because of the
word I have
spoken to you.*

JOHN 15:3

IN THE EARLY DAYS OF springtime the vineyard is at its best, tidy and uniform.

The labor of winter has left the vineyard neatly trimmed, each plant perfectly tied to the long, straight rows of glistening wire. The flexible new canes and miniature leaves are beginning to show, vivid light green—and spotless. The spring rains keep the dust at bay.

The farmer looks across his vineyard with a deep satisfaction at its beauty and order. Everything is clean, ready for the fruitful season ahead.

That is exactly how Jesus described his disciples as he told them the story of his Father's vineyard. The description came at an interesting moment, too. Jesus' first words to them about the vineyard had been about how the Father cuts off unfruitful branches and prunes those that are fruitful.

Like us, the disciples must have wondered where they fit in. What does he think of me? Am I about to be cut off?

So gently, Jesus pronounced their safety:

You are already clean! Don't worry about the Pruner's shears; it is not time for that. You are already neatly trimmed and fit for the season ahead.

Jesus wasn't asking fruitfulness of them that day. This was springtime, not harvest. They were simply ready for the process of fruitfulness to *begin*.

How had this state of readiness been accomplished in the disciples? By the *word* that Jesus had spoken to them. He had made them ready with the truth of the gospel he had expounded to them. As they responded to that gospel, it washed them and made them clean.

That is true of us, also.

Christ's word makes us clean, able to stand before God, radiantly adorned and blameless. Since fruitfulness arises only out of the depths of our friendship with Jesus, it cannot begin until we are comfortable in his presence, confident that we belong there. To have that confidence, we must be cleansed of our past sin, cleansed of our guilt, cleansed of our shame over past attitudes and actions.

Jesus declared his disciples clean and by so doing declared springtime in their hearts. Conversion is always our first spring. Nothing more aptly describes those who embark on a new walk in Christ! We begin in God's kingdom newly made. Our friendship with Jesus is established, and his voice and power become evident in our lives.

However, this is not the only spring we experience in the kingdom. There will be other times when God renews us with promise and vision. Their arrival may not be as predictable as springtime in the vineyard, but come they will when our lives are pruned and

> *Christ loved the church and gave himself up for her to make her holy, cleansing her by the washing with water through the word, and to present her to himself as a radiant church, without stain or wrinkle or any other blemish, but holy and blameless.*
>
> **EPHESIANS 5:25–27**

cleaned, prepared for the next work that God wants to do in our lives.

Yet here we differ greatly from the physical vines in the vineyard. They are only clean during one season, but we are called to be clean at all times. Each day, through our repentance, we can receive God's cleansing work. Each moment we can be confident of our access to God as we keep turning from our ways to follow him.

Each day, each moment, we can be as clean and new as the vineyard in springtime.

LIFE-GIVING NOURISHMENT

NO ONE WALKING THROUGH the peaceful vineyard in spring would imagine the vigorous process of nourishment going on deep beneath the scraggly bark of the vines. Through small capillary tubes, nutrients and water flow up through the roots, travel through the trunk, and spread out through every branch until they reach each leaf and maturing grape bunch. This life-giving sap makes the difference between a branch that is fruitful and one that is fit only for destruction.

The only time you can actually see this flow of nourishment is early in the spring, before the vine fully shoots. A small drop of sap hangs on the end of each trimmed cane. In the low-lined morning light these drops reflect like diamonds, a sure sign that spring is at hand.

The sap is what the vine gives to the branch to make it fruitful. In order to receive this nourishment, the branch must be part of the vine—not just nearby or hanging on. Likewise, we must be linked to our Lord in a way that nourishes our spiritual lives.

How can we know if that is happening? Jesus gave his disciples one sure test. "If you remain in me and *my words* remain in you." The nourishment he gives us is in the words he speaks to

If you remain in me and my words remain in you, ask whatever you wish, and it will be given you.

JOHN 15:7

us. If we are remaining in him, his words will fill our lives.

Jesus wants us to know who he is, what he is like, and what he is doing in our lives. He does this by revealing himself in two important ways.

The first of these should be most obvious—Scripture itself. Here is God's full revelation, recorded so that at any moment we can pick it up and know him more completely. Jesus inhabits Scripture, and every bit of it speaks of him. So if we want God's abundant joy and fruitfulness in all situations, we must cultivate a regular pattern of feeding on his Word—reading it, studying it, and learning to interpret it accurately.

Yet the "words" Jesus referred to that night with his disciples are not fulfilled by Scripture alone. The second way Jesus wants to reveal his life to us is by speaking to us personally. He still speaks today, through the Holy Spirit, and learning to recognize his voice is critical to a maturing friendship with him.

That God speaks to us through his Spirit does not devalue Scripture. Anything the Spirit speaks today will only apply the truths of Scripture to our immediate circumstances. Scripture, in fact, is the place where we learn to develop sensitivity to God's voice—to recognize his thoughts when he breathes them into our hearts. If our perceptions of God's voice don't square with Scripture, whether in content or intent, they can be soundly rejected, for God will never act in a way that violates what he has already revealed about himself.

There are always times when, despite our best efforts in prayer or study, we remain confused, unsure of the Father's will for us. We don't always recognize his voice, or it is drowned out by the clamor of circumstances, our fears, or our own desires. But if we immerse ourselves in his Word, letting the sap of his life run through us, we will learn to hear his voice with increasing clarity.

Where is Jesus leading me today? What is he teaching me? What attitude or carnal appetite is he dealing with, and how do I cooperate with him to see that work completed? The answers come by remaining on the Vine, learning to detect his continued presence. As we do that, gradually we find our desires transformed to match his. We grow so close to the Vine that we want what he wants—to have his life flowing through us.

If we remain in him and his Word, we will become more and more fruitful—and the sap will keep flowing.

A Burst of Springtime

*Let us go to the
countryside....
Let us go early to
the vineyards to
see if the vines
have budded, if
their blossoms
have opened.*

SONG OF SONGS
7:11–12

GRAPEVINES ARE NEVER the first to herald spring. The white blossoms of the almond tree and the vivid pink of the peaches break out much sooner. The vine takes its time, not willing to send out its tender buds until the danger of frost is far past. While other fruit trees are trumpeting their glory, the only change observed on the vine (and for this you will have to look closely) is the swelling of its buds.

Then one day, as if on cue, the vines suddenly explode into new life. Looking down the vineyard row you can see the faintest tint of green as the leaves curl out of the broken bud and aim skyward. The tender, pliable shoots are an iridescent green, almost transparent. Once begun, the vines grow eagerly, watered by the spring rains and coaxed out by the ever-warming sun. Soon a bright green canopy crowns the rows of vines.

Spring has come to the vineyard, and the forces of fruitfulness have begun their long and steady march to produce sweet, succulent grapes. Every leaf is fresh and clean, spreading out to catch the sunshine. Underneath, the tiny white blossoms emerge, promising a bountiful harvest.

Love, joy, beauty, promise—all are synonymous with spring.

It reminds me of our spiritual lives, of the times when we touch the presence of God at every turn, hear his voice with clarity, and find no circumstance too daunting for our faith. We look to the future with excitement and vision, confident in God's ability to bring our hopes to pass. Following on the heels of the cold, waiting days of winter, spring is eagerly welcomed. Each day is a fresh adventure in God's grace.

But as glorious as the days of spring are, they are also a time of danger. A late frost, a freak hailstorm, or an assault of weeds or insects can spell a quick end to a promised harvest.

It is easy to give in to the enemy's distractions during this heady time, to find the promises of God aborted because we become preoccupied with other things. It can happen to any of us. God prepares us to bear fruit, but just when he is ready to set it we allow it to be stolen.

It doesn't take much. A lingering need, a persistent sin, a major disappointment, or even an unkind word from another believer can destroy our joy if we let it. Some are distracted from the promise by an unhealthy preoccupation with God's gifts to them—an effective ministry, a promotion at work, or a new child or home.

Months later, we look back at the days of promise with frustration, wondering why God never accomplished what he had promised.

Yet all the time his Father-heart has not changed.

His purpose has always been our fruitfulness.

We are the ones who must follow through.

We must learn in the springtime how to cultivate God's work deeply in our hearts. Then, when the blossoms fade, we will stay with his work until the weak nubs at the end of our branches become glorious bunches of grapes.

I am the true vine, and my Father is the gardener.

He cuts off every branch in me that bears no fruit,
while every branch that does bear fruit he prunes so that
it will be even more fruitful.

You are already clean because of the word
I have spoken to you.

Remain in me, and I will remain in you.

No branch can bear fruit by itself; it must remain in the vine.

Neither can you bear fruit unless you remain in me.

I am the vine; you are the branches.

If a man remains in me and I in him, he will bear much fruit;
apart from me you can do nothing.

If anyone does not remain in me, he is like a branch that is
thrown away and withers; such branches are picked up,
thrown into the fire and burned.

If you remain in me and my words remain in you, ask whatever
you wish, and it will be given you.

This is to my Father's glory, that you bear much fruit,
showing yourselves to be my disciples.

As the Father has loved me, so have I loved you.

Now remain in my love.

If you obey my commands, you will remain in my love, just as I have obeyed my Father's commands and remain in his love.

I have told you this so that my joy may be in you and that your joy may be complete.

My command is this: Love each other as I have loved you.

Greater love has no one than this, that he lay down his life for his friends.

You are my friends if you do what I command.

I no longer call you servants, because a servant does not know his master's business.

Instead, I have called you friends, for everything that I learned from my Father I have made known to you.

You did not choose me, but I chose you and appointed you to go and bear fruit—fruit that will last.

Then the Father will give you whatever you ask in my name.

This is my command: Love each other.

John 15:1–12

*No discipline
seems pleasant
at the time,
but painful. Later
on, however, it
produces a harvest
of righteousness
and peace for
those who have
been trained by it.*

HEBREWS 12:11

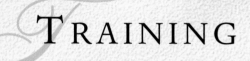

TRAINING

NEW SPRING GROWTH IN THE VINEYARD is so prolific that if left to itself it would sprawl out everywhere. Not all of this growth is good. Some of it merely siphons off the strength of the vine instead of adding to it. One of the most important tasks of the farmer at this time of year is to direct growth on the vine for maximum fruitfulness.

Part of this training process involves the mature branches. There are new canes called *suckers* that sprout from the base of a vine, drawing energy away from fruit production. These must be cut off. Sometimes even beginning grape bunches are plucked off to help the remaining ones grow larger and sweeter.

The most vital training, however, is that done with the new vines, those just entering their first growing season. The way the farmer trains these young vines will affect their fruitfulness for years to come.

The farmer begins by tearing off every shoot that grows from the leaf joints of the new vine. What he wants for the first year is a single long branch, with all the vine's energy concentrated on strengthening it. The following winter, he will prune that branch at a height that will allow next year's shoots to branch off from the top. Branches that appear lower on the trunk will again be plucked off to force the strength of the vine into the branches that will ultimately bear the fruit.

In the Father's vineyard, too, the process of training is vital to our spiritual growth. During our spring seasons, when growth is profuse, the Gardener works to align our lives with his plans. This process of alignment is known as *discipline.*

Without discipline, there would be no fruit.

So God takes our discipline seriously. He trains us, not by tying us to poles and wires but by calling us to obey his voice. He speaks through a message from Scripture, through a comment from a friend, or through his Spirit in our hearts. As we obey, we are shaped toward greater fruitfulness in our lives.

We accept his prompting to call a friend, and we are shaped toward loving sensitivity. We follow the biblical guidance not to respond to a hurt with another hurt, and we are nudged toward forgiveness and patience. We persist in a daily quiet time, and we find our connection to the Vine being strengthened. One act of obedience after another, we are trained toward fruitful maturity.

But we don't necessarily like it.

Discipline is not always comfortable—for the grapevines or for us. The training of a grapevine breaks the natural inclinations of a branch's growth, as does our obedience. Sometimes we feel as if we're being bent the wrong way.

So we resist. Like a vine being trained, we prefer to do what comes naturally. We rationalize our interpretation of God's voice to fit our own ambitions.

When that happens, the Gardener becomes a little more insistent. He may use our circumstances to bring greater clarity to his direction, and this can be even more painful, because our selfish pursuits and self-sufficiency are revealed for what they are—vain attempts to find life in ourselves.

But don't misunderstand. Although discipline may be uncomfortable or even painful, it is *not* punishment. Punishment, although it may have deterrence in mind, is still primarily retribution. When God disciplines us through uncomfortable circumstances, he is not enacting revenge—he is nurturing and guiding.

Discipline isn't legalism, either, although many have confused the two. It is not a set of arbitrary rules and regulations we must meet in order to achieve acceptance and status from God. Once we are chosen by Christ, we are already accepted, chosen. We don't have to earn our place on the Vine.

The Lord's discipline, remember, always has our *training* in mind. The purpose of discipline is to shape us according to God's desires and to direct our spiritual growth toward maximum fruitfulness.

In the early years, in fact, establishing a healthy growth configuration through discipline is even more important than producing fruit.

Every good grape farmer knows that's true for the vineyard. No vine will produce fruit the first year anyway, and there won't be enough in the second and third to make any difference. So during the first years, a farsighted farmer will pick off the bunches just after they have bloomed so that all the energy of the vine will go into rooting deeply and developing strong branches.

That's a good thing to remember in our lives as well, especially when we're new in the faith or when we feel that God is calling us to do a new thing. Sometimes the wisest thing we can do is wait, grow, and follow God's discipline instead of pushing ahead to achieve "results."

The best fruit always comes in God's own time, anyway—and in the appropriate season.

What To Do in Springtime

IN SPRINGTIME, the vineyard can almost take care of itself.

That is, it grows without really needing the farmer to take care of any of its immediate needs.

The rains water it.

The soil nourishes it.

The weeds are too small to provide any real challenge at this point.

So what does the farmer do in springtime, other than training the young vines?

One day he might be on his tractor, plowing down new weed sprouts or spreading fertilizer beneath the vines. This time of year he'll almost always have a shovel with him to scoop away small weeds from under the vine or to clip off a sucker.

The farmer, you see, is already looking ahead to summer, when the weeds will be much larger and can choke out the vine. The fertilizer will nourish the vine and strengthen it to endure the long haul of summer while the fruit ripens.

This is the time when the farmer sets a pattern of care that will sustain the vine through summer, when it will need to be

Seek the LORD while he may be found; call on him while he is near.

ISAIAH 55:6

> *This year*
> *you will eat*
> *what grows by*
> *itself, and the*
> *second year what*
> *springs from that.*
> *But in the third*
> *year sow and*
> *reap, plant*
> *vineyards and eat*
> *their fruit.*
>
> ISAIAH 37:30

strong and healthy the most.

So in our lives, in the season of great joy and promise, God invites us to establish patterns of relationship with him that will endure the severest tests of faith.

But too many of us cannot see the need. Everything is going so well just the way it is. Why do we need to let God deal with our fleshly desires, since he seems to be blessing us in spite of them? Why do we need daily time in the Word, since God seems to be speaking to us everywhere we turn?

It is precisely at times of great blessing, when God is so readily present, that patterns of spiritual relationship can be built most effectively into our lives. When God is easy to find—in our Scripture reading, our prayers, and our fellowship with the body of Christ—that is the time to set the patterns that will strengthen and prepare us for the days to come.

Though the Word emphasizes this pattern of preparation, many believers mistakenly think that their spiritual life will flourish regardless. They assume grace will cover spiritual lethargy. But whenever we decide we need just enough of God to survive the day, we have let the process break down. Our response to God today has implications months down the road.

Nowhere is this more powerfully illustrated than in the vine. Grapes are a two-year crop. The bunches forming now were developed a year before, while another crop was coming to fruitfulness. Although they were microscopic in size, hidden in the buds of next year's crop, the care the vine received then

determines their quality now.

Complacency is the greatest danger we face when God blesses us in the springtime. We don't need to participate, we think; God will do it all. How wrong that is! Whenever complacency grips our heart, we must call ourselves back to repentance. The Gardener is doing all he can to ensure a future nourished by his presence. We need to do likewise.

Almost always, long days lie between promise and fulfillment, and those are the days when the process of transformation takes place. When God is moving powerfully in our lives—that is the time we need to develop patterns of relationship for the future.

Now, while springtime is still here.

For spring will not last forever.

PART THREE:

I went past the field of the sluggard,
past the vineyard of the man
who lacks judgment; thorns had
come up everywhere, the ground
was covered with weeds,
and the stone wall was in ruins.
I applied my heart to what I observed and
learned a lesson from what I saw:
A little sleep, a little slumber,
a little folding of the hands to rest—
and poverty will come on you like a bandit
and scarcity like an armed man.

Proverbs 24:30–34

13

A TIME FOR MATURING

Let us not become weary in doing good, for at the proper time we will reap a harvest if we do not give up.

GALATIANS 6:9

IN THIS VALLEY, summertime tends to sneak up on you.

The other seasons trumpet their arrival: fresh green leaves in spring, red and orange leaves in fall, the first dusting of frost in winter. But summer slips in quietly. The days simply begin to stretch out, growing longer and hotter.

In springtime, the landscape of the vineyard changed almost daily. Fresh canes exploded from the vine, stretching to the heavens until their own weight caused them to curl earthward again. But now the expansive growth slows as the focus moves from the leaves to the tiny fruit beneath them.

The new grapes are about the size of BBs and almost as hard. Since early spring, when they were first formed, they have sat virtually idle while the leaves were deployed—solar collectors of the energy that will bring the grapes to maturity. Now, in their turn, the grapes begin to swell. By summer's end they will reach their full, sweet maturity.

These are days of hard work, far less beautiful than the blooming glory of spring, yet equally important, for these are the days of persevering—the time between promise and harvest. The farmer has settled into routines of irrigation and cultivation.

There is not much he can do now to increase the crop, but his neglect of these duties can certainly bring a swift end to it or severely damage its quality.

In our spiritual summers, between spring and harvest, so many believers lose hold of their hope in God. They see the glory of God's promise fade, because the fulfillment is not yet in hand. They give up, thinking that a promise delayed is a promise denied.

But the farmer doesn't see summer as a delay. He sees it as part of the process that brings the promise of spring to the abundance of harvest. His eye is firmly fixed on the formation of the fruit. Summer is not the end. It will not last forever—just long enough for the fruit to ripen. Although this season of heat is difficult, it is essential. So the farmer perseveres, not with resigned despair but in hopeful anticipation.

Our spiritual summers demand the same perseverance. We cannot jump from spring to fall. We must endure the trying days of summer, assured that perseverance will bring us to maturity, not destruction. We must meet the challenges of summer head on, for without the long, hot days there would be no harvest.

Scriptures praise the men and women of God whose faith traversed this chasm between promise and harvest. They endured the onslaughts of summer by drinking deeply of God's goodness and staying the course while the fruit ripened.

If we are going to be fruitful in God's kingdom, we can do no less.

14

*It does not fear
when heat comes;
its leaves are
always green.
It has no worries
in a year of
drought and
never fails to bear
fruit.*

JEREMIAH 17:8

DEEP ROOTS

I HAVE A NEW GRAPEVINE in my yard. It's a good four years behind the other vines. There's not one grape bunch on it—just one small, stately cane growing up the pole to the arbor above. This new vine replaces one that died last summer for lack of water.

You see, the San Joaquin Valley is an irrigated desert. It is a rare drop of rain that falls here between mid-May and November, so anything that grows here, including vineyards, must be watered.

My father irrigated his vines every three or four weeks, depending on the severity of the heat. And he didn't just sprinkle water on the surface; he deep-watered by flooding the fields. Deep-watering forces the roots to grow deep instead of loitering near the surface. This not only keeps them well-nourished until the next irrigation but also helps anchor the vines firmly and gives them greater breadth for drawing needed nutrients from the soil.

In Jesus' tale of the vineyard, of course, believers are likened to branches on a vine, and branches don't have roots. If we can shift our thinking for a bit, however, to see ourselves as vines rooting into the soil, we will see more clearly what we need to be doing in our spiritual summer.

In a farmer's way of thinking, if a vine dies for lack of water, it's the farmer's fault. He is responsible to provide sufficient water.

Spiritually, however, the responsibility for how deep our roots plunge belongs to us. God always provides sufficient water, but we must develop roots that go deep enough to absorb that water, to outlast the heat of summer.

Believers who spend little energy establishing their roots will demonstrate quick external growth. After coming to Christ they may busy themselves with Christian activities and services, and others may be impressed with their zeal and energy, but the long, hot summer is yet to come. Trials and difficulties can beat down on a believer with the same dry harshness as the sun on the vineyard.

These arid, brutal times are not an indication that our spiritual life has suddenly taken a downturn. They are simply another season of growth, part of the process of producing fruit. We prepare for them by developing a root structure—an abiding friendship with Jesus—deep enough to withstand any trouble or disappointment, any onslaught of doubt or fear. Roots that go deep are not affected by temporal circumstances. They can weather heat and pressure, drawing from God's life with the same joy as if it were raining in spring.

How do we develop deep roots? For a plant it happens quite naturally: The sun dries out the soil from the top down. As the abundance of surface water vanishes, the roots keep looking for it. So they grow deeper, where the soil has not dried out yet.

The same is true for us.

When worship at church seems mundane, instead of blaming the worship leaders, we need to seek God more fervently—past the goose bumps and the heart flutters, digging for the treasure of his presence.

When Bible reading or prayer time seems difficult and lifeless, instead of giving up, we can seek him more diligently, making sure it is our heart that is reaching out to him, not our works.

If our Christian fellowship has grown sour or stale, we can press through with honest sharing, humble forgiveness, and encouragement from the Word, so that our focus is centered on him.

In all our seeking, we must remember the Gardener. He has promised he will always provide enough water for his vines: "I, the LORD, watch over it; I water it continually" (Isaiah 27:3).

Roots that are fully developed provide continual refreshing, as if planted near a spring. With spiritual roots like these, we don't learn to get by on less of God; we find God at a deeper level and with greater consistency.

With deep-watered roots we never lack—no matter how hot and dry the summer.

FRUIT FROM THE HEAT OF SUMMER

15

THE CLOCK MOVES PAST NOON and the sun arches high overhead. The vines seem to shimmer as unrelenting ripples of heat soar skyward.

Day after day, the heat hangs as thick as a theater curtain and dead still, without a whisper of wind to freshen the stale, musty air.

Day after day, the vines endure the full force of the sun that beats down on this valley.

For the vines and farmer alike, the summer sun is a mixed blessing. To ripen, the grapes need a certain number of sunlight hours above seventy-seven degrees. In that sense, my father's vineyard is a perfect place to grow the sweetest grapes, since our arid climate rarely offers a cloudy day in summer. But the heat that accompanies these sun-filled days also stresses the vine. Too much heat can sap the vine of its strength and even diminish the quality of the fruit.

This is summer in my father's vineyard, and it models one of the great paradoxes of our faith: Fruitfulness rises out of a hostile climate.

Day and night your hand was heavy upon me; my strength was sapped as in the heat of summer.

PSALM 32:4

> *We also rejoice in our sufferings, because we know that suffering produces perseverance; perseverance, character; and character, hope.*
>
> ROMANS 5:3,4

In other words, the heat of trouble and persecution that bears down on us is precisely the environment God needs to bring our lives to mature fruition.

This clear message from the New Testament is often played down. Who wants to dwell on suffering when we can talk of prosperity, blessing, and the abundant life?

Yet every major voice in the New Testament underscores the reality that our faith flourishes in a hostile climate. None of the writers saw this as a cause for mourning. Quite the contrary. They were stirred to rejoice in the toughest of trials.

Jesus' teaching about the vineyard immediately precedes the most severe trial his young followers had ever faced. In the next few hours he would be betrayed and crucified. He warned them he was leaving them, and fear ran rampant in the room. Yet over and over he appealed to them, "Do not let your heart be troubled."

James picks up that same message: "Consider it pure joy, my brothers, whenever you face trials of many kinds."

Why? Should we put on a fake smile in the midst of pain, pretending that we're happy to suffer? No! Trials are a cause for rejoicing because of what they can produce in our character. Faith under test produces perseverance, and perseverance takes promise to completion.

We don't rejoice in trouble for trouble's sake, but we do realize that trials can purify our faith and increase our fruitfulness. Though the trial itself won't produce the fruit, our faith in the midst of it will. We have a choice—to respond in faith and let the trial mature us, or to respond with anger and let it defeat us.

God in his magnificent grace takes even our worst circumstances and makes them part of the maturing process. He will never let the heat of summer destroy us. He promises we will never meet a trial greater than we can endure. He provides a way to escape the evil in it and to overcome it by his grace.

Our challenge is to persevere—to keep coming to God in spite of our hurts, our doubts, our anger, to remain in the Vine, drawing on him for strength to endure the heat and trusting that the difficult circumstances we face will produce his fruit in us.

When you feel seared by summer's heat, that's the time to draw closer to God than ever.

And keep on thinking . . . fruit!

16

UNDER THE LEAVES

*This is
to my
Father's
glory, that
you bear
much fruit.*

JOHN 15:8

THERE'S NOTHING A GRAPE farmer likes to do more than peek at his crop, looking carefully between the leaves to see how the grapes are coming along and how big he can anticipate the harvest to be.

To this day, anytime between the first budding and the final day of harvest, I can ask my father, "How does the crop look?" and without hesitation he will have an answer.

"About average," or, "Looks like 15 percent above normal."

Even when the grape bunches are smaller than the eraser on my pencil he has already checked to see how many grapes fill those bunches and how many bunches hang from each vine.

That all takes some serious peeking—peeking that will continue even into the days after the harvest, just in case the harvesters missed one of the bunches. There is nothing more important to a farmer than the fruit growing in his field. After all, why else plant a vineyard?

Jesus tells us that his Father is no different. Everything the Father does in his vineyard is geared to making each branch on the Vine fruitful. That is his first priority.

Unfortunately, we haven't all come to the kingdom of God

with that same priority. Some of us came looking for freedom from fear, some for protection from temptation, some for comfort and security. And the Father offers us all these things. He meets us at the point of our deepest need, but he never leaves us there.

God has one priority in our lives—to make us fruitful. And since God's priority will carry the day, as long as we hold to any other objective we'll find ourselves frustrated with his work in our lives.

Now, saying that God wants us to be fruitful doesn't mean he doesn't want us to be fulfilled. Any farmer knows that fruit only results from fullness. What is best for the vine's life is also best for its fruitfulness, for fruit is simply the overflow of life. Even the uncomfortable process of discipline is undertaken in part so that we might know the fullness of joy that comes from being fruitful.

> *So, my brothers, you also died to the law through the body of Christ, that you might belong to another, to him who was raised from the dead, in order that we might bear fruit to God.*
>
> ROMANS 7:4

Yet, as much as God delights in blessing his children, the intent of that blessing is not just for our personal happiness. He blesses us so that we might be a blessing to others. The only priority that drives the Master of the vineyard is to bring us to fruitfulness. He will do whatever it takes to make that happen.

That's also why the farmer peeks so often. He is not just estimating the crop, but also assessing how that crop is doing. Is it maturing? Are there any pests, mildew, or diseases that could destroy that harvest? Is there anything he can do to help the vine to greater fruitfulness?

So it is with God and us: He watches over the fruit growing in our lives, carefully tending to its development and thereby ensuring the harvest that is to come. Nothing delights his heart more than finding his branches spilling over with fruit.

What kind of fruit is he looking for?

In Galatians 5:22, 23 Paul clearly lists the fruits God desires: love, joy, peace, patience, kindness, goodness, faithfulness, gentleness, and self-control.

The fruit God desires, then, is borne in our character. It is the transformation of our lives so that we reflect God's nature to the culture around us. The call to fruitfulness and the command to love one another are one and the same. "By this all men will know that you are my disciples, if you love one another" (John 13:35).

The fruit the father desires is the fruit of love. He wants to see his character filling our lives, spilling out like grape bunches on an overloaded vine.

When we love the way God loves, we are bearing the fruit of his kingdom. That's what he's been working into us through the long process of growth and maturity in the vineyard.

The fruit of the Spirit is not what we can make ourselves do for a moment, but what God makes us to be for a lifetime.

ENEMIES OF MATURITY

EVERY YEAR they catch me by surprise.

It begins with an air assault, and if I'm not in the backyard every day where the vines grow I don't even see them. Black moths flutter in over the fence, steal into the grapevines, and lay hundreds of eggs.

Days later the army hatches. Small yellow caterpillars with brilliant purple and black stripes fan out across the leaves, devouring them as they move. They leave behind only the veins of the leaves, eerie skeletons of life destroyed. In a few days they can reduce a beautifully arching cane of greenery into a vegetative boneyard.

Skeletonizers. Their name stirs up gruesome images. Yet these are but one of many enemies that prey on a vineyard as the fruit matures.

It sounds like spiritual summer to me, when the enemy rises up to destroy God's work. At the very time we are the most stressed, as vines are in the heat of summer, Satan rushes in to attack. And he rarely launches one offensive, but moves in on many fronts at the same time.

> *That Satan might not outwit us. For we are not unaware of his schemes.*
>
> 2 CORINTHIANS 2:11

Many believers, expecting the joys of spring to last through harvest, are left unprepared for this onslaught of conflict that summer brings. Discouraged by the difficulties, they give up, cast off their fruit, and hope for better days ahead. Then when harvest comes and they have no fruit, they wonder why God doesn't use them.

To guard the growth of our fruit, we need to recognize how the enemy comes to destroy our fruitfulness and then rebuff his every attempt.

During summer, the attacks will come at three different levels. First there are enemies that attack the roots, the lifeline of the vine. That's where unchecked weeds take their toll, as do nematodes, worms that live as parasites on the roots. Our friendship with Jesus is always in the enemy's sights. He schemes how to dislodge our affection and attention from our Lord. Anxiety and worry, greed and envy, comfort and complacency—any of these can be effective tools of the enemy in cutting us off from our lifeline.

The assaults aren't limited to the roots, however. A host of insects and mites can attack the leaves. To me the leaves represent that which takes God's life and makes it fruitful in us—our obedience to him. The enemy will do all he can to impede that obedience with temptation and distraction. He will incite our selfish ambition, pride, and trust in our own wisdom—all of these chewing at our responsiveness to God's work in us.

Finally, the enemy may attack the fruit itself. Fruit flies, worms, birds, and mildew all assault the grapes in my father's vineyard. Similarly, as the spiritual fruit of our lives ripens, the enemy launches a full frontal assault to destroy it. Just as we're learning love, patience, and kindness, he orchestrates circumstances to discourage and defeat us—to convince us that we will never be fruitful in our spiritual lives so we might as well give up.

In the Father's vineyard, there is one certain cure for almost any point of destruction: *repentance*. If we will humble ourselves before God, he will thwart the enemy's attempts and forgive us any complicity in allowing the enemy to gain footholds in our lives.

Unlike the vines in my father's vineyard, which cannot defend themselves, we play a key role in resisting the enemy's hand by recognizing his attempts and refusing to fall victim to his lies. Whenever he tries to weaken our relationship with God, to distract us from simple obedience to God or discourage our efforts to show the fruits of the Spirit, we need not let him succeed.

Instead, we must keep firmly attached to the Vine. Then we will have nothing to fear because God the Caretaker is our ally in this battle.

Make no mistake.

It's war out there during the hot days of summer. But we are not alone in the fight. And there is no doubt about the outcome when we cling to the friendship God has extended to us.

THE FARMER'S DILIGENCE

The sluggard craves and gets nothing, but the desires of the diligent are fully satisfied.

PROVERBS 13:4

FARMING IS NOT like writing a book. You don't spend a few years of diligent effort, achieve a finished project, and look back on it for years to come. Farming is a matter of doing the same tasks year in and year out, repeating them again and again to bring the vineyard to succeeding years of fruitfulness.

Almost as quickly as the farmer plows the weeds down in a row of vines, new ones begin to grow. They too will have to be cut. As soon as a pest is expunged from the field, its cousins are already infiltrating. A farmer clears a field and plants his crops in it. At that very moment the war is launched. The wilderness will forever seek to reclaim the land taken from it.

To be fruitful in God's kingdom, we too must be diligent to guard against the forces that seek to drive us back to the wild. We can't stand still in the life of God—either we are growing or we are withering away. Those who think they can merely hold their own are fooling themselves. Nothing in creation stagnates without dying.

But what does diligence mean in the vineyard? It doesn't necessarily mean working every minute, but it does mean doing what needs to be done *when* it needs to be done.

My father used to get up at five-thirty in the morning to sulfur his grapevines before the winds came up. I'm sure he would much rather have done it at ten, but it couldn't be done then, at least not effectively. Many times I've seen him leave a party he was hosting in his own home, put on his work clothes, and go out to check the irrigation. When it's time to irrigate, you can't wait just because it's the Fourth of July or the family reunion. When the water is running, it has to be checked.

Our spiritual life is just as demanding as the vineyard. It needs to be tended to *when* it needs to be tended to. We cannot set a regimen for our lives that will work through every season. Instead, we have to know by the Spirit's leading what is needed *today*. And that may not always fit smoothly into our schedule. We might even have to say "no" to something good to embrace something far better.

Diligence means doing what needs to be done *when* it needs to be done.

A farmer in the vineyard is always looking at the vines, noting their needs, combating their enemies, and keeping them watered. To be fruitful in the Father's vineyard requires the same watchful care. Daily we present our lives before God, looking for areas of the enemy's attack, lack of nutrition, or creeping attitudes that might draw us away from the Lord. Having seen any of these, we invite God to deal with them quickly to bring resolve and maintain our fruitfulness.

However, we must be careful here not to get trapped in an exercise of unhealthy introspection. We don't have to spend endless hours contemplating all that might be wrong with our spiritual lives. God is our Caretaker, remember. He will show us where our attention needs to be drawn and what we need to do to continue the process of fruitfulness. All we need to do is listen and obey.

Diligence is simply a matter of doing what the Spirit wants you to do every day, without excuse or delay. Those who fit Jesus in only where it's convenient, or who can easily be distracted by the demands of this world and the expectations of friends and family, will sacrifice their spiritual growth.

God never intended that our spiritual life be our *first* priority; he wants it to be our *only* priority. When we give it that place, we'll find direction and strength aplenty for fitting in the things he wants of us at home, on the job, and even in our recreation.

At whatever cost, we must do that.

If we cultivate God's life in us with the same diligence that the farmer exercises in his vineyard, God will do his part in bringing us to full fruition.

HAVING DONE ALL, STAND

THE SUMMER COMES SLOWLY to an end. It is only two weeks until harvest. The vineyard is in its final stages of production. The fruit is ripening, making measurable gains in sugar content every day.

Here in the most critical days before the harvest, where would you imagine the farmer to be? Vigilantly prowling his fields? Battling the unending armies of insects or weeds? Fretting about unseen troubles that may be lurking out there?

I'll tell you where my family was in the beginning weeks of August: We were high in the Sierra Nevada Mountains, camping.

Unbelievable, isn't it? But there really wasn't anything for Dad to do in those last few weeks. Whatever he hadn't done before this moment wasn't going to make a difference anyway. The field was watered, and the vines were sulfured to keep out the mildew. It was too late to spray for insects; at this point the insecticide would only hurt the fruit. And no weed could grow tall enough in two weeks to challenge the vine. By this time the fruit was going to ripen no matter what we did. So we went camping.

A good farmer has a firm grasp of where his work ends and God's begins. The farmer can only do so much. He can water,

After you have done everything... stand.

EPHESIANS 6:13

cultivate, fertilize, and prune, but he cannot make anything grow—not one bunch of grapes, not one leaf.

Only God can make things grow.

That's also true of the fruit in our lives. We can sow and we can reap, but we cannot make one thing grow. To know the peace of God even in the most difficult circumstances, we have to know where our responsibilities begin and end.

We are not responsible for results in the vineyard—God is. All we need to do is trust him, and God will see to it that his purposes are accomplished.

That is the key to patience, and the best farmers are patient farmers.

My father is the most patient man I know. Whether being a farmer produced this in him or whether he chose farming because it fit his temperament, I don't know. But my father has a keen sense of what is his responsibility and what is God's—and he flatly refuses to take over God's.

When the rains came and destroyed his crop one harvest, his faith in God never flinched. I would have lain awake at night fretting or pacing the patio and rebuking the storm, but I never saw my dad do any such thing. Instead, he simply threw up his hands, cocked his head with a smile, and said, "What else can I do?"

We could all learn to use those words more—not in frustration or anguish, looking for desperate alternatives, but in the simple recognition that we have done what we've been asked to do and the rest is in God's hands.

Only God can make things grow. You learn that in a vineyard. City life reinforces the ridiculous notion that if things aren't going our way it's because we aren't trying hard enough.

Be patient, then,

brothers, until the

Lord's coming. See how

the farmer waits for the

land to yield its

valuable crop and how

patient he is for the

autumn and spring

rains. You too, be

patient and stand firm,

because the Lord's

coming is near.

JAMES 5:7–8

Do you know how many believers live in the bondage of that kind of thinking in their spiritual lives? Every time something goes wrong, they blame themselves. So they redouble their efforts, thinking that if they can just do more, maybe things will turn out their way. It's not true. Some things we can do, some we can't.

When you work with growing things, you have to be patient. You have to do your part and let God do his and try not to get the two confused.

We can't expect God to plant or weed, since he wants us to do that, but neither can we make the branch grow or the fruit ripen. That's his part.

Whenever I read Ephesians 6, I think of those August vacations. "After you have done everything . . . stand!" When you've done everything you know to do, even if circumstances aren't coming out the way you thought they would, just wait. God will go beyond your abilities to accomplish his purposes.

He wants us to trust him and not confuse diligence with prevailing by our own efforts. Our task is to abide in the Vine. If we do that, following whatever God shows us to do, he will be free to accomplish everything he has chosen to do with our lives. I see too many people at the threshold of the promises God has made to them who just can't wait until the final work is done. They grab for a more immediate substitute, only to discover later that it falls far short of God's promise.

Sometimes the best thing to do is just to stand firm—to wait patiently for God to do his work in our lives.

It might help to throw up your hands and smile peacefully: "What else can I do?"

SOFTER AND SWEETER

Take my yoke upon you and learn from me, for I am gentle and humble in heart, and you will find rest for your souls.

MATTHEW 11:29

THE HARVEST is almost here!

By early August, the clusters of fruit are hanging heavy on the vine. They weigh down the branches, straining the support wires. Each round grape is swollen to full size. Each looks full and juicy, and the temptation is strong to pull one off and pop it into your mouth. Can't you just taste the succulent sweetness?

If you did that now, though, you would be in for a sour disappointment. For if you were to pick a grape from the vineyard today, the tartness would pucker your lips, and the hardness would set your teeth on edge.

The grapes look ripe, but they're not ready to harvest yet. It will take a few more weeks of maturing for the fruit to turn soft and sweet.

In the final days before harvest, the leaves are working hard to pump the grape bunches full of sugar. Almost daily you can taste the changing sweetness as the sugar content soars. This influx of sugar also softens the pulp inside the grape. In another week or two, when you bite through the firm outer skin, the juicy sweetness will explode in your mouth.

When that happens, you know the harvest is at hand.

The same things that signal the maturity of a grape signal the maturity of a believer. One of the sure signs that God is bringing his promises to completion in our lives is the softness and sweetness that floods our spirit and our demeanor.

Early in our spiritual walk, in the midst of promise and struggle, we might find our spirits hard, full of arrogance. We find ourselves fighting and striving in our own efforts to accomplish God's work. But later we discover that summer yields its best fruit in the final days before fulfillment, when God changes our hearts, softening them with humility and gentleness and sweetening them with lovingkindness.

The ripe fruit of the Spirit—love, joy, peace, patience, kindness, goodness, faithfulness, gentleness, and self-control—are the signs of a person who has been transformed by God's presence. This is the fruit the Father has been watching for all along.

But, in all honesty, these are not the attributes most desired or encouraged by the world around us. How does the world regard a person who exhibits these traits? A wimp? Perhaps a codependent? Whatever the description, it isn't a compliment.

No, the world system is clear: If you want to make it, you have to be tough. You have to know what you want and grab for it, because no one is going to give it to you. You must show no sign of "weakness"—that is, kindness or gentleness—because someone is waiting to take advantage of you the moment you do.

Those are the rules. Everyone who succeeds learns them early and follows them adamantly.

Everyone, that is, except Jesus.

Jesus' life demonstrated an inner peace that others could not destroy. He was kind to the outcast and took advantage of no one, not even his own disciples. In every conflict he faced, through every lie directed against him, he demonstrated the gifts of the Spirit. Yet no one that we know of ever called him a wimp. In fact, many people were frightened by his authority, though he never enforced his will on anyone.

Softness is not weakness, even though the world might call it so.

In God's kingdom, softness and sweetness are measures of strength as well as markers of maturity.

Even the disciples failed to understand this fact at first. James and John wanted to call down fire from heaven when people in a Samaritan village wouldn't extend hospitality to Jesus. They were ready to usher in God's promise the world's way. "We'll show them who's boss."

I can just see Jesus smile as he shook his head. *Still kids,* he thought. Just like a farmer who bites into an early August grape—"No. They're not quite ready yet."

But eventually they did learn the lesson. That same John was the one who repeated over and over again those simple and powerful words of Jesus: "Love one another."

The end product of summer, for those who persevere in faith, is a gentle and humble spirit. There is no more accurate sign of maturity than treating others, all others, with kindness and gentleness.

When sweetness settles on your heart, you know that summer is over.

And then . . . let the harvest begin!

PART FOUR

Never again will I give your grain
as food for your enemies,
and never again will foreigners
drink the new wine
for which you have toiled;
but those who harvest it
will eat it and praise the LORD,
and those who gather
the grapes will drink it
in the courts of my sanctuary.

ISAIAH 62:8–9

TIME FOR A CELEBRATION

TO THE GRAPE FARMER THERE is no scene more thrilling than swollen grape bunches cascading out of the leaves like billowing fountains.

All the efforts of the past year have aimed toward this moment.

But as beautiful as that sight is to the farmer, the scene is not as idyllic as it might sound. The vines sag under the weight of the fruit like tired, swaybacked horses. The leaves are ragged and frayed, dulled by a heavy cloak of dust. Some have yellowed; others have wilted completely. Many have pieces ripped away, tattered reminders of summer's warfare.

The vineyard is not particularly beautiful this time of year— except to the farmer. To him, its beauty lies in its fruitfulness. The long struggle is over, and the vines have won. The grape bunches, bulging with sweetness, testify to this success.

Harvest is at hand. God has brought another crop to completion.

And that is cause for rejoicing.

Although I never enjoyed farmwork as a child, some of my fondest memories include the last ride on the tractor from the fields to the barn. The trailers were stacked as high as possible, trying to make each trip the last. The sun-ripened grapes formed a mountain, sloping down to the edges of the box.

The harvest was gathered. We had beaten the winter storms for another year, and now the crop was safe. The hot, dusty work was over.

I remember on more than one occasion surveying the awesome sight of rows and rows of boxes stretched out across the top of the hill near the outbuildings. A year's worth of labor and all my father's income for an entire year lay stacked in the boxes on that hill.

The last act of harvest was always a celebration. Shouts of joy, song, and laughter filled the air on that final ride home. Afterward we would clean up and enjoy a magnificent meal—a feast to celebrate the harvest and the gracious God who had made it all possible.

Celebration is just as much a part of the vineyard as diligence and perseverance.

Not surprisingly, harvest and celebration are closely connected throughout Scripture. In an agrarian society that predated cold storage and prepackaged food, the harvest was next year's lifeline. At harvest time, the previous year's food supply, paced to last through the entire year, would be running low. That's not easy for us to grasp when our supermarkets are loaded with food every day of the year. How can we recognize the vulnerability of the harvest when we can replace a frost-devastated citrus crop in California by shipping oranges from Florida—or vice versa?

For a society without such luxuries, harvest was a time of fervent celebration and thanksgiving. In fact, God ordained two feasts to bracket the harvest. The Feast of Harvest came at the beginning, when the precious firstfruits were offered to God in thankfulness for another crop. The Feast of Ingathering marked the successful completion of the harvest itself.

Both were to be celebrated before God. He, not nature, had provided bountifully for the year to come. His faithfulness was truly cause for rejoicing.

Those of us who see the Father's hand in the harvest rejoice, our hearts filled with joy. But we rejoice even more in the spiritual harvest. Out of our broken lives God brings forth the fruit of his kingdom. Can you see it in your life? From your branches hang sweet fruit—love, peace, patience, gentleness, and self-control. Lessons learned. Changes made. Relationships healed. Hope restored.

It is all *his* doing.

That's why we mark it with celebration.

Fruit Doesn't Lie

In every grape, the history of the vine is told.

If it was a good year and the vineyard was properly cared for, the fruit will burst with sweetness. If the vineyard was neglected, the fruit will be small and tart.

Fruit doesn't lie.

The truth of a branch's life is found in the harvest. The branch that remains in the Vine will reap an abundance of fruit, useful for the Master in extending his kingdom. His character, developed in the branch, will demonstrate his love and grace to others.

However, there is a less joyful side to the harvest. The branch that did not pursue friendship with Jesus wholeheartedly but neglected spiritual nourishment will face a sad reality at harvest: puny fruit or perhaps no fruit at all.

If we resisted the Master when he sought to train us to the wire or we cast off our fruit in the weariness of summer's heat, the harvest will reveal what has happened. If we stayed just close enough to Jesus to survive, our fruit (if any) will be pale and tasteless.

Worse yet, if we only pretended to draw life from Christ but in fact resisted his work in us while serving ourselves, our fruit

By their fruit you will recognize them. Do people pick grapes from thornbushes, or figs from thistles?

MATTHEW 7:16

will bear our own likeness and not his.

Fruit doesn't lie. It expresses the life of the vine. That's why Scripture views the harvest in both positive and negative terms; it demonstrates the quality of our lives, whether good or bad.

Fruit cannot be faked. Though we may be able to pretend a godly attribute for a brief season, in weak and tired moments our lives will reveal our true choices, priorities, and attachments.

Fruit makes the invisible visible. It shatters all pretense and over time marks the true depth of our friendship with Jesus.

Don't expect grace to cover up your neglect by producing spiritual fruit. Grace restores us to God's presence. Grace forgives our sins and offers us a fresh start. But grace will never produce fruit when we have not paid the cost to remain in the Vine. It will not make up for the times when we have given in to the enemy's deception.

Fruit doesn't lie. When it finally appears, it reveals what has been going on in the vineyard through all the seasons. And God's harvest is often full of surprises.

The people we thought were pursuing God may not turn out to be his followers at all.

The activities and pursuits in our own lives may turn out to be fruitless—or they may produce the joyful confirmation that we remained on the Vine.

In the time of harvest, only one thing matters—our friendship with Jesus.

And the depth of that friendship will be measured by the fruit we bear.

The fruit of the Spirit is love, joy, peace, patience, kindness, goodness, faithfulness, gentleness and self-control. Against such things there is no law.

GALATIANS
5:19–23

FRUIT AND SEEDS

Look at the fields! They are ripe for harvest.

JOHN 4:35

YOU PROBABLY DON'T THINK much about it when you sink your teeth into a delicious piece of fruit. As the sparkling sweetness explodes in your mouth, it is easy to forget that the fruit is also a seed.

The earliest passages in Genesis tell us that God created fruit for this dual purpose—food to be eaten and seed to be sown. This is true also of our friendship with Jesus. As he shapes us into his image, the fruit of our spiritual lives draws others into his kingdom. Because their unregenerate hearts cannot behold the invisible God, they need to see him first in us.

How will they know his love if we don't love them?

How will they understand his gentleness and forgiveness unless we demonstrate it?

How will they know he is faithful unless we are faithful to them?

The fruit of our lives has its greatest use when it demonstrates the reality of God to others. During days of harvest, not only do we celebrate what God has accomplished in us, but God also uses us to touch others.

In other words, harvest time is ministry time—the time when the fruit of our lives is invested in the lives of others.

Harvest ministry begins when we take a co-worker to lunch, when we run an errand for a neighbor, or when we offer a listening ear to the man standing next to us at the bus stop.

Whenever another human being is warmed by our love, uplifted by our hope, disarmed by our patience, inspired or unsettled by our faith—that person encounters the life-giving reality of the gospel. From these encounters other branches are grafted onto the Vine, and the joy of the harvest grows.

The most effective work of the harvest is not accomplished through sermons or evangelistic rallies or institutional outreach or even through Christian books. Yes, these things can be expressions of ministry and God often uses them to bring people into his kingdom, but they are not the heart of harvest ministry.

The heart of harvest ministry is people encountering people. It is people whom God has changed reaching out to people who are rejected and hurting and hungry for meaning in their lives.

That is not to say that ministry is automatic—even for branches who are abiding on the Vine. We still have to make the choice to share our fruitfulness. There will be plenty of times when we would rather do almost anything than help a neighbor or talk to a hurting child.

But something interesting happens when we do choose ministry.

We find that the very process of ministry furthers our growth on the Vine. The more God shapes us in his likeness, the more our ministry opportunities increase. We have more opportunities to obey, and the harvest increases.

Fruit and seeds, remember, are part of the same process, and relationship with Jesus is key to producing both. If we want to keep living fruitfully on the

Vine, harvest ministry is not an option.

How do we do it? By not limiting our activities to the safely religious. By cultivating relationships with unbelievers at work and in our neighborhoods. Through these relationships, God will show himself to the people who need him. We don't need to force the issue. We just need to stay close to him, and we'll find his love overflowing into the lives of others.

A branch does not harvest itself, remember; the Gardener does. He's the One who is in charge of the harvest. Our job, both as fruitful branches and as harvest workers, is to remain on the Vine.

We can depend on God to do the rest.

No Harvest?

CAN ONE EMBRACE the promises of God in spring, endure the perils of summer, and still come through the harvest with no fruit to show for it?

This happened to my father at least twice that I can remember. Unseasonal rains in September rotted his entire crop of raisins while they were lying on the ground to dry—a whole year's labor wiped out by one freak storm from the subtropics. Other dangers can have the same results; insects or birds, for instance, can settle on a crop and devour it completely.

The enemies of fruitfulness don't give up just because fall has come. My father never considered his crop safe until it was delivered to the packer. Only then could he relax.

Can a crop be lost in the Father's vineyard? Can we faithfully pursue God with all our heart, only to have fruitfulness snatched away from us at the moment of promise? I think not. But if I don't qualify that statement I'm afraid you'll misunderstand.

The reason I would say no is because Isaiah's words are so clear: "As the rain and the snow come down from heaven, and do not return to it without watering the earth and making it bud and flourish, so that it yields seed for the sower and bread for the eater, so is my word that goes out from my mouth: It will not

Though the fig tree does not bud and there are no grapes on the vines, though the olive crop fails and the fields produce no food . . .yet will I rejoice in the LORD, I will be joyful in God my Savior.

HABAKKUK 3:17–18

return to me empty, but will accomplish what I desire and achieve the purpose for which I sent it" (Isaiah 55:10, 11).

As long as we continue to remain in the Vine by remaining in Christ's Word, our lives will indeed bear fruit.

And yet—the fruit our lives bear may not be the fruit we anticipate.

Many of us carry unrealistic expectations of what our fruitfulness may mean. We confuse being fruitful with being successful in the world's eyes or living in comfortable bliss.

We couldn't be more wrong.

Take Stephen, for instance. He was among the first believers in the early church to emerge with a powerful and fiery ministry. Yet just as he was coming into his own, he was stoned to death. To some, the life of Stephen may seem like a harvest aborted. Yet his life did indeed bear fruit—not only in the witness of his life and death, but in the eventual witness of a man who watched his execution, a man who would one day be called Paul.

If we remain in the Vine, God will be faithful to produce fruit in our lives. But not all our fruit will be borne in ease or even in this life. The obstacles of this world and the assaults of the enemy will provide constant challenges. Yet even though our circumstances may not always come out as we expect, we can always expect God to be glorified through us.

Don't look to your circumstances for the measure of your harvest. You simply cannot trust your perceptions of them. There are only two ways a harvest will be aborted in our lives as believers: if we give in to the enemy's devices and give up our faith in the midst of difficult times or if we suffer God's judgment because of rebellion. This happened to Israel at times, and will happen to us if we abandon God. But he always preserves the harvest of those who remain on the Vine—even if the harvest comes in unexpected forms.

What does all this say about my father's failed harvest? Did God wipe it out because of rebellion? No! Whether the enemy thwarted Dad's harvest, or whether he was simply a victim of capricious weather, what was really at stake was his faith.

And here's where I learned more about faith than in any other single experience.

The first time God didn't stop the rains, I watched my dad carefully. I saw him one afternoon staring out at his field, the rain pelting down in sheets. An inch of rain had already fallen on the drying grapes a few days before, damaging them severely. This second storm would spell their end. He knew that. I saw the helplessness and disappointment in his eyes, and I felt as bad for him as I've ever felt for anyone. Didn't God care? How could he let this happen?

"What are we going to do, Dad?" I asked, wondering how we would eat in the coming year.

Through his disappointment his response was clear: "The Lord is faithful." After a long pause, "We'll just have to see how the Lord will provide for us in the year ahead."

And provide he did. We didn't miss any meals that year. But more important than that physical provision was the unforgettable lesson God gave me through my father's faith.

Crops can be lost. Circumstances in our life can be troublesome, even devastating. But they are just crops. They are just circumstances. They needn't destroy our fruitfulness for the kingdom.

After all, this is our Father's vineyard. He alone is our strength—and he is powerful enough to bring us through any circumstance, all the while making us more fruitful for his kingdom.

Don't Stop Growing

THE HARVEST IS winding down in my father's vineyard.

A few fat bunches of grapes still hang from the branches, but most are already spread on the racks to dry into luscious raisins. The branches are spent, depleted by the effort of ripening the fruit. The leaves are bedraggled; the vines seem to sigh with relief that the growing season is finally over.

But it isn't over. Not yet . . .

Even with the harvest drawing to a close, the vines, branches, and leaves are still at work, taking up moisture and nutrients from the soil and drawing on the sun's rays to convert those nutrients into usable nourishment.

The sap is still flowing.

The branches are still growing.

The growth that happens now, in fact, is just as crucial as the growth of spring or summer.

What the vines are doing now, you see, is storing up strength for the fruit of seasons to come. This part of the growth process will continue until the very last days of fall, when the leaves finally wither and fall to the ground.

The cycle of the seasons doesn't end with the harvest.

Let us live up to what we have already attained.

PHILIPPIANS 3:16

In fact, next year's grapes are already being formed in the buds of the first-year canes. If the branch were to let down now, next year's crop would be impaired.

The nutrients produced now will not be needed in the coming winter because the vine will go dormant. They will be stored in the trunk and the roots to be available next spring when the branch explodes with new life. When the new leaves are not strong enough to produce their own nutrition, they will live off what the vine stores now.

"Remain in me."

There is no season when the branch can afford not to heed that admonition.

In fall as much as in summer, our diligence to walk with Jesus and follow his voice must remain our priority, although in days of fruitfulness this may seem less urgent. We cannot allow ourselves to think that just because we are being used to extend his kingdom, we can get by without being nourished by our relationship to him.

So don't stop growing, even during the harvest times of your life—perhaps especially during the harvest times. Cherish his presence and go to him often to replenish your life in him. Allow your relationship to deepen. Listen to his voice and let him show you what he is doing in you beyond the harvest itself.

For every harvest, you must remember, is part of an ongoing series of harvests. A vineyard does not bear fruit once and then die. Even when the fruit is being gathered, there are yearnings and visions stirring for crops still to come. Throughout our lives there will be many seasons of fruitfulness. So don't be surprised if one season of harvest doesn't fulfill all your dreams and visions. God will bring you to another season, and still another beyond that—until the day when the final harvest comes and his reapers bring history to its conclusion.

Here we know in part and see in part. But one day the perfect will come. Then we will come into the full fruitfulness for which God chose us from the beginning.

If we could see our lives that way, no amount of suffering could thwart us, no pain could overwhelm us. God is preparing us for all eternity in his presence. What we have valued most in this life of eternal consequence is being saved for us there.

The branch is now ready for the winter. Its storehouses are fully replenished. The euphoria of harvest ends, but the door is open to an even more wondrous season beyond.

You can already feel the chill in the air.

Winter is at hand.

PART FIVE:

Be at rest once more, O my soul,
for the LORD has been good to you.
For you, O LORD, have delivered
my soul from death,
my eyes from tears,
my feet from stumbling,
that I may walk before the LORD
in the land of the living. . . .
How can I repay the LORD
for all his goodness to me?
I will lift up the cup of salvation
and call on the name of the LORD.

PSALM 116:7–13

FADING GLORY

*Forgetting
what is behind
and straining
toward what is
ahead, I press
on toward
the goal....*

PHILIPPIANS
3:13–14

AFTER THE HARVEST, the glory of the vineyard seems to fade quickly.

The leaves turn yellow now; they have finished their task. The nutrients not used this year have been stored for the next. The vineyard is closing down, preparing for dormancy.

Here in the Valley, winter usually steps through the door with its first freeze in the waning days of November. Then rest comes quickly to the vineyard as the leaves turn brown and fall earthward.

Early winter does not showcase the glory of the vineyard. The vines look shriveled and barren. Stray bunches of rotted grapes hang limply, uncovered in winter's nakedness, and debris fills the rows between the vines. Some canes have broken off, while others fall loose, split open by the weight of the ripening grapes.

It's not easy to watch God's glory fade—in the vineyard or in our lives.

It's even harder not to do anything about it.

But this is the season to let the glory go.

To be a good branch on the Vine, we have to do only two things. First, we need to remain in the Vine, treasuring friendship with Jesus every day. Second, we need to let go of everything else, even the success of the harvest. Serious disciples must learn the secret of letting go. God moves on, and he invites us to go with him—even into the season of winter.

When the apostle Paul summarized his guiding passion for life and ministry in Philippians 3, he said simply that it was to know Christ. Everything else in comparison was rubbish. Then he added what every branch needs to learn: Forget the things that lie behind and press on toward the prize of God's highest calling. Paul was not referring just to failures and sins, but to successes and joys as well.

Never is the danger of simply hanging on greater than at the onset of winter. The harvest is a time of euphoria, with almost daily opportunities to touch lives. We watch God do amazing things through us, temptations are far distant, and even our most difficult moments are swallowed up by an overreaching joy.

Yet like all seasons, harvest runs its course. Suddenly the opportunities aren't as laden with power as they had been; they are fewer and farther between. We don't seem as effective as we used to be. We have to redouble our efforts just to get by. Temptations return with a vengeance, and every little thing that goes wrong irritates us.

What has happened? Why is the joy slipping away?

It's easy to panic if we don't recognize that a new season has begun.

Our first conclusion may be that something is wrong with us—that we have failed or disobeyed. We try repentance, but it doesn't seem to be the answer. While it might refresh our walk with the Lord, we still watch helplessly as the harvest withers. What are we to do?

Most of us try to hide the fading. If we don't let people see it, they won't know the harvest is over. So we cover it up, most commonly with busyness. We push through by our own efforts what had seemed so graced before.

But that's not the way it happens in the vineyard. No farmer holds onto the harvest, hiding its end lest someone think him a failure. Every farmer celebrates not only the harvest, but also its conclusion. In fact, I've never met a farmer who wasn't *relieved* to have the crop in and winter approaching.

The onset of winter is not to be lamented—far from it. These are days when the vineyard will be restored for a new year. The activity of growth slows, so the farmer has time to tend to other needs in the vineyard.

No season of ministry is open-ended. God harvests in specific seasons through specific people. If we recognize this fact, we can allow specific harvest times to come to completion—and then we can celebrate and let go.

The early church did that. Paul and Barnabas went on their first outreach through Asia and then came back because "they had been committed to the grace of God for the work they had now completed."

No, not everyone in Asia had been touched. Not every problem had been solved. But that particular harvest time was over for Paul and Barnabas. Their task was done. They could celebrate it and move on to other things Jesus wanted them to do.

This is the Father's vineyard, remember. He is in charge of the harvest; he has planned what will happen season by season. One branch was never meant to bear all the fruit in the vineyard or to live in continual harvest. So when opportunity around you slows, when you don't seem to be as effective as you had been, when God seems a little distant, it may be time for a change of season. And if you have a hard time letting go, perhaps you need the coming winter more than you know.

Now is the time to shift your attention away from developing fruit and spreading leaves to that vital link between vine and branch. If you have the courage to set aside the good things God has brought to completion in your life, you will have more time and energy to devote to your friendship with Jesus.

These are the best days for personal retreats and extended time in the Father's presence. As things grow quiet, you'll see more clearly his direction in your life—perhaps discover some less-than-pure motives that have sneaked in during the growing season. Don't resist this process, even if it feels that you've failed or that you're wasting your time. Spiritual winter provides the Father opportunity to do an even deeper work in your life.

Don't look for fruit in winter. You will be sorely disappointed. But do pursue your friendship with Jesus, and you will find that winter is a wonderful season to enjoy him.

You will understand that your leaves and your fruit—your productiveness and your activity—are not your glory. Your true glory is the depth of your friendship with Christ.

And regardless of the season, that's a glory that will never fade.

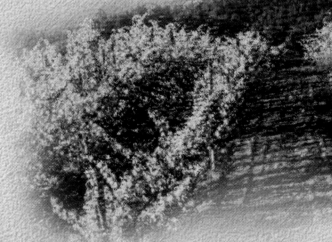

The Colder the Better

WHAT IS MORE SERENE than the earth under a blanket of freshly fallen snow?

Nature has come to a standstill. The only sound is ice crunching underfoot. People speak in muted tones.

The stillness is almost deafening.

I've felt that same stillness in my father's vineyard. Instead of snow, a low, gray overcast swaddles the vineyard with silence. The vines stand quiet, twisted forms frozen in time. No more work is done, not for the time being.

For the vineyard, this is a season of rest. Summer was the season of warfare, of battles to protect the fruit from hostile forces. Fall was a time of vigorous harvest and celebration. Now the cold of winter lulls the vines to a much-needed quiet.

God does this with us—but not because he turns cold and unresponsive. Quite the contrary, it is during this season of rest and restaging that God draws even closer to us, placing a greater priority on our relationship with him and his Son.

There are two ways that God brings us to winter. One is circumstantial, where the external trappings of our spiritual life become less effective. The second is by calling, where God directs

*Be still,
and know
that
I am God.*

PSALM 46:10

us to lay things aside and concentrate for a time on our relationship with him. Both signal an end of one season of fruitfulness in order to prepare for another.

There are many instances of such seasons in Scripture. The time Moses spent on the back side of the desert changed him from a prince in Pharaoh's court to an ambassador and a deliverer for God. The children of Israel spent forty years in the wilderness—a winter season when God forged a people who could occupy the Promised Land and be fruitful.

Jesus retreated to the wilderness after his baptism. There God prepared him for his public ministry. We don't know all that happened in the wilderness, but Luke tells us that Jesus went out full of the Spirit and returned in the power of the Spirit. Jesus recaptured similar moments when he withdrew from the crowds to lonely places for prayer.

Because of these examples the winter season is often referred to as a wilderness experience. That designation is fine, if by *wilderness* we mean a time when God calls us to a season of undistracted attention away from the busyness that ensnares us. But I've heard many people define the wilderness as a time when God withdraws his presence from us to deepen our faith. Nowhere does Scripture suggest such an idea. God wants to increase our dependence upon him, not teach us how to live without him. When the old patterns grow lifeless, he beckons us to a fresh discovery of his love.

The rest of winter is not the result of burnout. The vine is not wasted from its fruitfulness. On the contrary, it has more strength reserves at the end of fall than at any other time of the year. In my father's vineyard, if autumn was particularly dry he would give the fields one last irrigation.

*Justice will dwell
in the desert and
righteousness live in
the fertile field.
The fruit of
righteousness will be
peace; the effect of
righteousness will be
quietness and
confidence forever.
My people will live in
peaceful dwelling
places, in secure
homes, in undisturbed
places of rest.*

ISAIAH 32:16–18

This ensured that the dormancy was part of the normal growth cycle not the result of carelessness or starvation. A healthy vine rests while a starved vine withers, and the distinction between these two, though not always evident in winter, will be obvious next spring.

No, winter is not burnout, but God drawing us to the quiet, where he does his deepest work. I've never heard it explained scientifically, but every farmer knows that the colder the winter, the better the crop next year. Mild winters lead to average yields. It seems the further the sap is driven into the vine, the richer its return.

The more we let God slow us down, and the more we let him put us on the sidelines, the more empowered we become for the days ahead.

We need to welcome the stillness, for only then can we hear the depths of God's heart and find his true leading.

 Pruned

28

IT IS THE MIDDLE of winter. The dried leaves in the vineyard have all fallen, and only the canes remain. The sap has slowed to nearly a standstill.

Now the farmer's winter labor can begin. There is one major activity to attend to in winter, and it is the only one out of the entire year that is specifically highlighted in John 15. That's not surprising, since nothing will have more impact on the health and fruitfulness of the vine than *pruning*.

Most of the time the farmer cares for the vine by protecting it from insects and elements that could destroy it, but in pruning he cuts and shapes the vine to make it as fruitful as possible.

My father particularly hated to hire outsiders for this job. Hasty and careless pruning can ruin a vine for seasons to come. So on cold winter mornings during Christmas break and on weekends, my father would take his four sons into the vineyard. Bundled up against the cold, we could barely move, but with pruning shears in hand we followed him into the fields.

A vine in winter is a confusing array of tan canes that uncoil from the vine like broken watch springs. Emerging the

He cuts off every branch in me that bears no fruit, while every branch that does bear fruit he prunes so that it will be even more fruitful.

JOHN 15:2

previous spring as flexible green spirals, they have now become woody sticks that shoot out every which way. Along the length of each cane, small brown buds about half the size of a pencil eraser grow several inches apart.

Inside these little buds, bunches of fruit for the coming year have already formed. Each bud contains one primary bunch, fully formed, albeit at microscopic size. Each bud also contains one or two secondary bunches that will sprout if something damages the first.

The problem is that there are too many bunches for the vine to carry successfully to harvest. Each cane holds twenty to twenty-five buds, and there are anywhere from forty to sixty canes on each vine. So the excess canes must be cut off.

Snip. Snip. Snip. The shears tear into the vine, reducing the number of canes to just five. That's all the vine will be able to support in the coming year. The sheared canes are stacked in piles and dragged to the middle of the row, where they will be chewed up as compost. In a rather short period of time the vine is radically transformed from confusion and chaos into a simple, stately form with five canes arching gracefully into the winter sky.

The pruning process is not without discomfort for the vine. Where canes are cut off, open wounds remain. They will heal soon enough though, because the sap is not flowing (thus is not draining the vine's strength), and diseases and pests that could infect the wounds are dormant. That's why pruning can only be done safely in winter. To prune the vine without damage, it must be done after the sap has slowed and the vine is at rest.

Damage? Yes, pruning is organized destruction. It is surgery of the highest order, and unless the branch is at rest when the process begins, this cutting could destroy it.

If a vine is pruned correctly, its growth will spread out evenly. It will carry the right amount of fruit to term, and its shape will facilitate the care it needs through all of the growing season.

What a marvelous picture of the surgery God performs in our lives! He prunes us so we can bear more fruit. He cuts away the clutter from our lives. Yes, it wounds us, but these are the wounds of a friend who cuts softly and tenderly. And he prunes us while we are at rest, in an environment where we are being refreshed by his presence, so the wounds are not so painful nor so likely to be used by the enemy to engender bitterness or rebellion.

And so he cuts. First, to rid us of canes that are broken or unhealthy. God cuts away the worldly passions and distractions that siphon off our spiritual life. During pruning we will have a keener sense of our sinfulness because he is calling us to repentance. He prunes carefully, making sure there is no area where the enemy can keep a foothold.

Second, God cuts to rearrange our lives under his agenda. Growth and harvest have a way of multiplying opportunities in our lives, but those opportunities can spread us so thin we are fruitless. They can also distract us from our friendship with Jesus. The pruning resets our focus so we can concentrate on what he wants us to do rather than everything we can do. Better to do a few things that are fruitful rather than lots of things that are futile, things that turn out to be empty foliage.

Fruitfulness, not busyness, is the goal of a conscientious believer. "The grace of God . . . teaches us to say 'no,'" Paul wrote to Titus—no to the worldly passions that destroy us and no to the opportunities that overwhelm us. Notice it is not fear that teaches us to say no, but *grace*. Because we can trust God and know that he will lead us into the fullness of joy, we are free to say no even to the things that we desire, whether good or bad.

There's just too much going on for us to participate in all of it. We've got to limit ourselves and focus on the few things God really has called us to do. That's the only way to be fruitful. We must draw near to God in the quiet season and let him show us his plans. His grace will teach us to say no.

The life that listens to God is not a whirlwind of activity, but a focused life. God's pruning results in simplicity, power, and joy. It brings fulfillment and fruitfulness.

Don't resist it.

It's the key to your fulfillment and fruitfulness.

29

TIED TO THE WIRE

Everyone who competes in the games goes into strict training. They do it to get a crown that will not last; but we do it to get a crown that will last forever.

1 CORINTHIANS 9:25

A LONG, SHINY WIRE runs the length of each row in the vineyard. It is a simple but lifesaving tool: it supports the canes above the vine so they won't break under the weight of foliage and fruit in the new season.

All of that fruit weighs a significant amount. If the canes were not supported by the wire, the weight of the fruit would cause them to split or break off from the branch. The fruit would be lost—the cane a victim of its own success.

So the last thing the farmer does in winter is to wrap the five canes on each vine around the wire. Two canes now run down the wire in one direction, and three in the opposite direction. When a row is tied on the wire, it looks like one unending cane stretching the length of the field. Everything is in a tidy, straight line.

Tying is a challenging task for the farmer. The canes are almost a year old now and not nearly as pliable as they used to be. Their rigid, woody grain resists the farmer's attempts to curve them back to the wire. They try to slip from his grasp, protesting by popping and snapping as he reins them in.

The farmer must be careful. If he pulls a cane too abruptly

or at the wrong angle it will break off, and one-fifth of the crop of that vine will be lost. The farmer must be infinitely gentle, curving the cane carefully back to the wire in an arc that will not break.

The cane, of course, would rather remain free, reaching out to the heavens unrestricted by the wire. Right now it doesn't need the support. But by the time it does—when the leaves are thick and the fruit begins to ripen—it will be too late. It will be impossible to wrap the cane on the wire then without breaking off most of the new growth.

Like the vines in my father's vineyard, we too need support for our fruitfulness. All too often we sense God's calling in our heart, and then set out to accomplish it in our own way. Though we may find some measure of success, the biblical fruitfulness we anticipate never comes. Unless our calling is reinforced with godly support, that will always be the case.

The history of the body of Christ is littered with people who were not strong enough to withstand their own successes—people who started out remarkably fruitful, only to be pulled under by pride or sin or some other failure. Behind each tragic incident is the story of someone who stepped out unsupported in spiritual growth and fruitfulness.

You need support if you are going to be a fruitful branch in the Father's vineyard. You need the support of his presence as you touch him in prayer and in his Word. You also need the support of other believers—Christian brothers and sisters who will come alongside you in prayer and honest dialogue. They can help confirm the validity of what you are hearing and encourage you to put your confidence in the Father—while you, of course, do the same for them.

With these supports you can rest confidently, knowing that God will be able to complete his work in you.

Take hope; winter is now almost over. Rested and reshaped, the vineyard is ready for another season of growth.

This is where we began many pages ago. We've come full circle, for spring with its burst of joy and freshness is once again just around the corner.

A new year is about to begin, and through it all, Jesus' lesson in the vineyard continues to resonate. He is the Vine. We are the branches. Our Father is the Gardener, and his purpose, always, is for us to "go and bear fruit."

When all is said and done, what matters is the fruit—borne for the kingdom of God, ripened by our friendship with Jesus, and expressed in our transformed lives.

He is fully capable of leading us to that.

For this is my Father's vineyard.

*A*ND MY *F*ATHER IS ALWAYS *F*AITHFUL.

I have told you
this so that my joy
may be in you and
that your joy
may be complete....

My command is
this: Love each
other as I have
loved you.

JOHN 15:11–12